Notes From A Small Island

🐚 🐚 🐚

Ellen Kort

Poems by
Ellen Kort

Illustrations by
Jeffrey Hargreaves

Fox Print, Inc.
All Rights Reserved

Acknowledgements

"Great Blues" was published in the **Wisconsin Poets' Calendar**, 1994, Wisconsin Fellowship of Poets.

Notes From A Small Island copyright (c) 1994 Fox Print,. Inc. All rights reserved. No portion of this book may be reproduced in any manner without written permission of Fox Print, Inc., except for excerpts contained in reviews or critical articles.

Published by Fox Print, Inc.
101 West Edison Avenue, Suite 247
Appleton, WI 54915
1-800-FOX-TALE (800-369-8253)

Poems by Ellen Kort
Illustrations by Jeffrey Hargreaves

ISBN 1-885520-00-X
Printed on recycled paper
First Edition, 2,500 copies

Table of Contents

Five Ways Of Listening To The Wind ...4
Within The Circle Of Moon, Turtle 6
Notes From A Small Island 8
Nothing I Name 10
Artist 11
Great Blues 12
Island Widow..14
Walking On Water..................................16
The Last Mile Flying 18
Feeding Fish At Alburys 20
Wind...21
Settled..24

Five Ways Of Listening To The Wind

All night this island moves
raucous wind
rattling the length
of her old bones

Hinge made of wind
rubs its voice
against the house

Articulate wind
settles nothing
argues buttonwood and tamarind
against sky   discusses
itself in the dark hum
of voice snarled in rock
until I am named by noise
by the contortions
its body makes   singing

Trees change shape
chanting a native tongue
casaurinas sway
loose hair in the wind
I feel their green pulse
in my left arm

All night   all night
the wind climbs into my bed
slides under my skin
separates flesh from bones
Hung as I am on this wind
I ride it out till morning

Within The Circle Of Moon, Turtle

This is how I see her
dark green shadow
making her way to shore
rising up
from sea light
Front flippers toss sand
cover shell until
only eyes thread
moonlight into
cleansing beads of tears

This is how I see her
sister
wild eggs
in her belly
sacred story
clotted with stars

letting go of fullness
slow brush of sand
over eggs   final
frenzied churning
that spreads
the ancient scent
of what she carried
how it rocked inside her
in the watery sea
and now
the long journey back

Notes From A Small Island

The moon is a yellow fist
fighting its way up through
branches of sea grape trees
It's a trick of the eye
the way it climbs over
this island   past the sail shop
one-room school   past
the post office   as though
it could live the rest
of its life here   rocking

back and forth like an old
woman who no longer leaves
her house   This island
spreads itself out   A narrow
street climbs the slope
from the boatyard   past
paintbox houses   paths lined
with conch shells   hibiscus
bougainvillea   until it reaches
the cemetary and the story

of a mother dying   how her
family took turns caring
for her   singing hymns
how she mouthed them
even as her eyes closed
When she died they rang
the iron bell and the men
in the boatyard stopped work
built a coffin of Abaco pine

A procession of people
carried her to the cemetary
remembered how years ago
wind-tossed waves raged
swept up and over the beach
clawed at graves   pulling them
out to sea   They spoke
of the gravity of water
all those names sailing into the wind

Nothing I Name

I saw lights in the sea last night
as I sat on dark huddle of rock
Water magic   Phosphorescent plankton
Ballet of lights leaping   Silver
blue dancing as if all the fireflies
of childhood had come out to play
Bits of stars tiptoed   flew   Nothing
I name could match the shiver of light
that peeled back dark skin of night

Artist

His eye holds the horizon
Sweep of arm follows water
into first light   color
so pale it twists inside
our throats   brushes
back and forth   hardens
Absolute blue begs the eye
open wide   takes us inside
green trees   to curve
of boat   weathered house
His hand releases the familiar
shape of an old man   back
turned   breath slow as rock
warm and wet as rain

Great Blues

Night sky
begins its meltdown
into green underbelly
of the harbor
Waves sing anecdotes
about the wind
abrasive words
heavy-hung with water

Three blue herons
lift up past the dock
undo a knot
of landscape   ancient
weavers unbraiding
the casaurinas

We watch slow pulse
of wings   purple
gray   soft cinnamon
Their colors visible
at close range
turn ashen   then black
as crows when long legs
push into the wind

Tomorrow I'll see them
standing in water
one-legged   waiting
But I'll remember
how they look tonight
great blues circling
in flight   waltzing
in and out of the sky

Island Widow

Pale as a gull's breast
she stares out from small
square house   held prisoner
by wind   too much sun
legs gone bad   Phlegm puddles
the back of her throat

Boats go out and return
Wherever they sail or anchor
she has been   She closes
the window against night
can still see him slice
into conch   as if her own

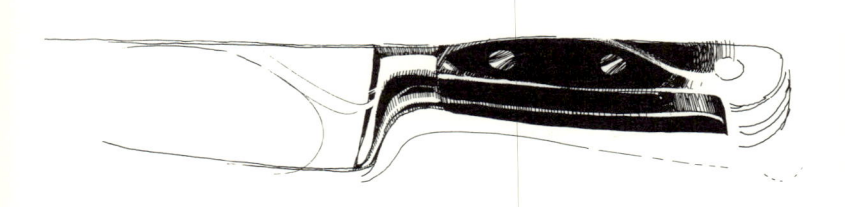

hand held the knife   how
easily he slid all those years
into hearts of trees   carving
tables   rockers   She spends
darkness counting names
Some are boats
or children

or maybe dogs who bark outside
her walls   She thinks of him
now   a coco-plum seed
buried in his hand   And
the tree   How it grew
Its roots hugging his bones

Walking On Water

You know how it is sometimes
when you look out on water
smooth as a mirror   I've always
wanted to try it   so I simply
stepped off the dock when
everything was clear and still
It wasn't like flying or
sleep-walking   But the surface
wasn't hard as glass either
and it wasn't like parting
the Red Sea or anything   I think
it was just a matter of wanting
to do it   putting one foot
in front of the other   and going

I went all the way around
the island   and when I got back
this friend of mine asked me
where I was and I said   "Out walking"
Now that I know I can do it
I can hardly wait until tonight
When the moon comes up
and makes a path on the water
I know exactly where I'm going

The Last Mile Flying

When she can no longer
see the moon   she leaves
the city   goes back
to her island of purple
sky and twisted shells
chooses for company
the sound of fish dreaming
blue sheaves of heron

She drops her duffle bag
on the dock   walks The Narrows
to Corn Bay where everyone
hears her one high trembling
note like a long howl of wolves

She gathers wild sour sop
and guavas   curls into
the beach   studies slant
of moonlight on slick rock
sings into sea-glass bottles
floats them to Cherokee
Little Harbour   Cat Island
or sells them to tourists
She rides the mailboat
writes letters about how
strong the wind blows tonight

Feeding Fish At Alburys

I lean over the railing to watch
grey snappers   a small barracuda
needle and trigger fish
swim stories up through water

They nibble   surface eat blue-
green morning   A woman hands
breadcrusts to a group of children
They bite off corners   spit them
out   lips making a perfect O

Fish   each with its own bright
flash of greed   open wide
And in that one moment I can see
a life   full of too many mouths

Wind

Six days ago wind started
as a smudged rubbing   limp
and soft   a charcoal shadow
in half light   scraping
against tree tops   extravagant
music hovering   flute-like
Wood-tap tambourine   leaf-singer
drummer   a silk-bright
dancer   legs and wings

Now when she turns to face us
she is some kind of mad body
all teeth   spitting   spinning
in one direction then another
wrapping herself in blue-black
clouds   She lets such finery go
as she comes flying across
the harbor   yelling and screaming
She calls in the rain   rears up

turns on herself   bangs into
the house   rams the boat dock
claws the shore   Roots hold
their breath   A bird flies like
a crooked stick   is stopped
for a moment   the sky's
dangling participle   Water rolls
back on itself like a conch shell

then floats quietly like two
middle letters of a word
spreads sky all over the ground
douses red fire from hibiscus
spills seeds   throws a palm branch
against the shed   Wind disguises
herself in footsteps   a knock
on the door   windows slam shut

🐚 She smells like everything she's
rubbed up against   wet feathers
bruise-colored moss   clam's
watery eye   soft flesh of mud
Listen   She whimpers now
clinging to the house
like a child   rocking back
and forth   begging to be held

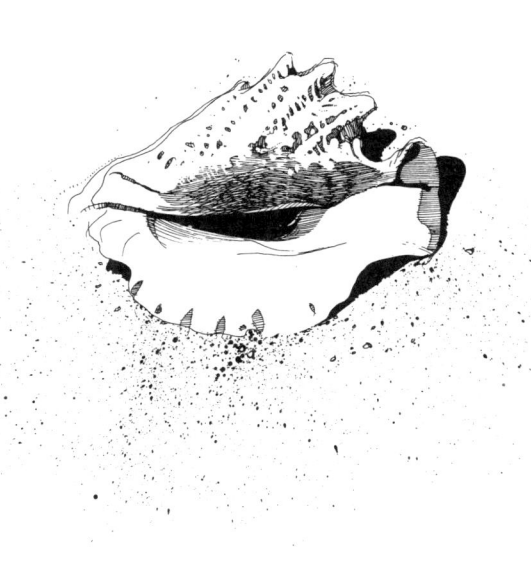

Settled

After late-night supper
of fresh crawfish
and homemade bread
we sit at the table
read to one another
nothing else in our lives
but rattle of leaves
and an island cat
begging at our door

Ellen Kort, a winner of the Pablo Neruda Literary Prize for Poetry, is the author of 11 books and has been featured in a wide variety of journals and anthologies. Her poetry has been set to music and showcased as performance pieces in concert and on stage. She lives in Appleton, Wisconsin, and is Director of Writing Services for an advertising agency. She also presents poetry readings and Creative Writing, Inner Awareness and Mask-Making workshops throughout the United States, Australia, New Zealand and the Bahamas.

Jeffrey Hargreaves is an award-winning illustrator who also does murals and a wide variety of portraiture. He has served as an art instructor for elementary students and is convinced that his childhood drawings of whales with big teeth inspired him to explore the world of art. He is Creative Director for an advertising agency and makes his home in Appleton, Wisconsin, with his wife, a daughter, a son and a cat.